The World's Best Gardening Jokes

In this series:

The World's Best Dirty Jokes
More of the World's Best Dirty Jokes
Still More of the World's Best Dirty Jokes
The World's Best Irish Jokes
More of the World's Best Irish Jokes
Still More of the World's Best Irish Jokes
The World's Best Jewish Jokes
More of the World's Best Jewish Jokes
The World's Best Doctor Jokes
More of the World's Best Doctor Jokes
The World's Best Dirty Stories
The World's Best Dirty Limericks
The World's Best Dirty Songs
The World's Best Aussie Jokes
The World's Best Catholic Jokes
The World's Best Mother-In-Law Jokes
The World's Best Russian Jokes
The World's Best Fishing Jokes
The World's Best Salesman Jokes
The World's Best Computer Jokes
The World's Best Scottish Jokes
The World's Best Cricket Jokes
The World's Best Golf Jokes
The World's Best Maggie Thatcher Jokes
The World's Best Lawyer Jokes
The World's Best Business Jokes
The World's Best Holiday Jokes
The World's Best Acting Jokes
The World's Best Drinking Jokes
The World's Best Gardening Jokes

The World's Best Gardening Jokes

Charles Alverson

Illustrated by Graham Morris

ANGUS & ROBERTSON

A division of HarperCollins *Publishers*

AN ANGUS & ROBERTSON BOOK

First published in the United Kingdom by
Angus & Robertson (UK) in 1991
A division of HarperCollinsPublishers Ltd
First published in the Australia by
Collins/Angus & Robertson Australia in 1991
A division of HarperCollinsPublishers
(Australia) Pty Ltd

Angus & Robertson (UK)
16 Golden Square, London, W1R 4BN
United Kingdom
Collins/Angus & Robertson Publishers Australia
Unit 4, Eden Park, 31 Waterloo Road,
North Ryde, NSW 2113, Australia
William Collins Publishers Ltd,
31 View Road, Glenfield, Auckland 10,
New Zealand

Typeset in Great Britain by New Faces, Bedford
Printed in Great Britain by
BPCC Hazell Books
Aylesbury, Bucks, England
Member of BPCC Ltd.

British Library Cataloguing in Publication Data
Alverson, Charles
The world's best gardening jokes
I. Title
828.91402

ISBN 0 207 16872 5

To Clare Alverson and Valerie Richards, sterling researchers

The wife came out into the overgrown garden and found her husband lying on the sun lounger.

'Isn't it a perfect day, darling?' she said pointedly. 'The sun is lovely and warm. A nice breeze keeps it from being *too* warm, and the song of birds keeps it from being too boring. Wouldn't it be a good time to get some gardening jobs done?'

'It's even more perfect than that, sweetheart,' answered the reluctant gardener without stirring. '-Someone has stolen all of my tools.'

The sales rep at the Gardening Show was having a terrible time. A very healthy crowd of potential buyers assembled in front of his pitch, but that was the only thing which went right. His company's sprays didn't spray; their new-model edger refused to edge; and the pride and joy of his company's new line, a computerised home Rotavator, started smoking as soon as he pushed the starter.

Hurriedly turning the machine off, the salesman looked into the expectant faces of the crowd and said: 'Well, that concludes my demonstration of the sort of problems you can have with *other* makes of equipment. At twelve noon, I'll be back here showing you exactly

what *our* new line can do to improve your home gardening.'

'I can't help wondering,' said one greenfly to another, 'whether there's life on other rose plants.'

An enthusiastic gardener is someone who will slave for twelve hours on a hot, sticky Saturday or Sunday and think all the time how lucky he is that it isn't a *work* day.

'My husband's an invertebrate gardener,' one woman told another.

'Don't you mean *inveterate*,' asked the other.

'No. *Invertebrate.* When it comes to the heavy work, he's simply got no backbone at all.'

The gardening contractor was estimating a job in a prospective customer's back garden when he broke off to look over the fence into the next garden to shout: 'Green side up!'

He went back to talking with the customer only to rush back to the fence and shout: 'Green side up! I told you, green side up!'

'What's that all about?' asked the bewildered householder.

'It's nothing serious,' said the gardening contractor. 'Just that I've got a crew next door laying a lawn.'

Asked why he'd stuck artificial flowers in between the rows in his garden, the gardener answered: 'You never heard of role models?'

'. . . and so you see,' concluded the lecturer at the gardening club, 'plants respond to loving kindness and react negatively to destructive thoughts. Are there any questions?'

'Yes,' said one of the members. 'Why doesn't that work with my weeds? The more I hate them the better they grow.'

One member of our Gardening Circle had terrific luck at shows because of his speciality of cross-breeding common garden vegetables. Year after year, he came back with awards for his turnip/sprouts, carrot/aubergines and tomato/cucumbers.

But this year the hybrid specialist came back from the show very glumly with no awards at all.

'What happened?' somebody asked.

'Oh,' he said, 'I guess I outsmarted myself at last. This year I thought I'd be very clever and cross sweet corn with parrot seed. It was a fine looking plant, but every time the judge tried to give his opinion, it kept shouting: "Rubbish! Rubbish!" '

The garden centre was having no luck at all shifting a consignment of sunflower seeds until the manager thought of putting a sign over the display: 'Van Gogh suffered torments creating his *Sunflowers*. An American collector paid £24 million for them. Here's your chance to do it the easy, cheap way – only 45 pence a packet.'

The caterpillar clinging firmly to a leaf near the ground watched as a white cabbage butterfly

soared overhead and was heard to tell a friend on the next leaf: 'You'd never get *me* up in one of those things!'

Summer is the time when the designers of seed packets are proven to be either blind optimists or out and out liars.

An old but very keen gardener consulted a spiritualist.

'Look in your magic crystal ball,' the old man said, 'and tell me whether there are gardens in heaven.'

'Very well,' said the spiritualist, and he stared into his softly glowing crystal for the longest time.

'Well?' said the old gardener impatiently.

The spiritualist looked up from his crystal and said: 'I can tell you that in heaven there are the most magnificent gardens. There are no weeds, and the ground is so fertile that seeds hardly have time to settle in the ground. Cherries grow as big as baseballs, and one carrot is enough for a meal for six. But it's not all good news.'

'What else?'

'Just as you interrupted me, I saw a twenty-foot high aphid with a spray gun.'

Feeling a bit adventurous, Norbert planted a bamboo plant in his otherwise ordinary garden. To his delight, it took off like a rocket and soon loomed over the rest of his plants. But as the exotic plant continued to reach for the sky, he began to worry that it was throwing his carefully planned garden out of proportion.

After several days of worrying, he finally called the faculty of the local horticultural college and asked one of the professors: 'What would be the effect if I cut a bit off the top of my bamboo plant to sort of, you know, integrate it with the rest of my plants?'

'Hmmm,' said the professor. 'Hang on a moment while I consult some of my colleagues. We're on our coffee break now.'

The expert was gone so long that Norbert thought that he'd been forgotten, but then the professor was back on the line.

'Sorry to keep you waiting,' he said, 'but we had quite a discussion on your question before we came up

with what could be the answer.'

'And what's that?' Norbert demanded a bit impatiently.

'It seems to us,' said the expert cautiously, 'that you would have a shorter bamboo plant.'

As an articulated lorry was rounding a curve, one of the huge logs it was carrying fell off and rolled clear across a wide lawn, stopping only a few feet in front of the house belonging to a keen gardener.

Hearing the unusual noise, the gardener opened his front door and enquired: 'What on earth is *that* doing there?'

'I'm not sure,' said his wife coming up behind him. 'Perhaps it's that new assemble-it-yourself garden shed you ordered.'

Sign on a newly planted front garden: 'Please stay off. I want to be a lawn.'

Trying on the skimpiest of bikinis before her mirror, Norma asked her husband: 'What do you imagine the neighbours would think if I went out and did the gardening wearing *this*?'

'I imagine,' said her husband without thinking, 'that they'd think I'd married you for your money.'

Lord Whatsis was out working in the walled garden when Jenkins, his head gardener, not paying attention to what he was doing, dumped a huge bag of manure so near to his lordship that it nearly crushed him.

'Jenkins, you're fired,' shouted his lordship. 'You nearly killed me.'

'Please, sir,' begged Jenkins. 'Give me another chance!'

'Don't you think it's a bit early to be planting those bulbs?' one gardener asked another over their common back fence on an unseasonally fine day.

'Well, yes,' said his neighbour, leaning confidentially over the fence. 'I know that and *you* know it's too soon, but I'm hoping that the bulbs don't know it.'

The proud gardener took his first lettuce of the season in the house and made a tremendous green salad. Just as he was going to tuck into it, his son said:

'Dad, are caterpillars good to eat?'

'What sort of thing is that to talk about at the table, especially when I'm just about to eat this beautiful salad?'

'But, Dad . . .'

'You heard me. We'll discuss it later.'

'All right.'

A little while later: 'Now, what was that you were asking me about caterpillars?' he asked the boy.

'Oh, never mind,' said the boy. 'There *was* a big fat one in the middle of your salad, but it's gone now.'

'When my son turns 21 next month,' said our gardening club chairman proudly, 'I'm going to give him his own key – to our mini-tractor.'

One spring, the neighbourhood handyman put an ad in our local news agents: 'Don't kill yourself in the garden this year. I'll do it for you.'

DONT KILL YOURSELF IN THE GARDEN
- I'LL DO IT FOR YOU

The gardening club bore decided to make his speciality the lowly ant or 'nature's natural gardeners', as he called them. Cornering a new member, the bore ranted on and on about the cunning tricks the ant world gets up to. 'Why, do you know,' he finally said, 'that these marvellous little creatures even have their own army and police force?'

'*Very* interesting,' drawled the newcomer, adding, 'no navy, I suppose?'

Two neighbours were terrific gardening rivals. The competition heated up until they weren't even on nodding, much less speaking, terms.

Finally, growing uneasy with this worsening situation one gardener rang the other's bell one evening with a pot of jam in his hand.

'What's this?' asked his neighbour suspiciously.

'A present,' said the other. 'I wanted you to have this pot of my Poached Raspberry Compote.'

'Why, that's very kind of you,' said the householder, defrosting markedly. 'I've never heard of such a thing. How do you make it?'

'The recipe is a bit of a secret, old man,' said the caller, 'but the name derives from the fact that most of the raspberries are from *your* side of the fence.'

'Show-off!' shouted one bee to another flying high over the flower garden.

'Why do you hate George so?' another bee asked as they drank from the trumpet of a morning glory.

'Oh, I don't know,' said the first. 'I suppose it's his "busier than thou" attitude.'

The suburban gardening society was quite pleased when a famous if slightly florid actor applied for membership. The more competitive members were even more pleased when the new member turned out not to be all that good a gardener and entered in several monthly shows without winning a single prize.

But then came a competition when the actor surprised everybody by bringing in a beautiful hydrangea of such size and splendour that it swept the boards. Everybody congratulated the actor except Ernie who, up until then had been the reigning hydrangea champion.

'Don't be a poor sport, Ernie,' someone said. 'Old Rex beat you fair and square with that magnificent specimen.'

'Fair and square?' snorted Ernie. 'I wasn't *beaten*. I was hambushed.'

If the sun produces such a terrific amount of energy, why does weeding out under it for only a couple of hours make one feel so tired?

The business executive duly collected his pension and gold watch and settled in to a new routine of staying at home. He seemed quite happy, and his wife was delighted to have him at home but as the days passed, she became more and more worried. Finally, she could hold it in no longer.

'Darling,' she said, 'you've been retired for two weeks now. Isn't it about time you started ordering seed catalogues?'

Notice on a suburban church notice board: 'Remember, this Sunday is our annual blessing of the power mowers.'

'What are the members like?' asked the new recruit to the local gardening club.

'It's hard to describe them easily,' said an old stager, 'but perhaps I can give you an example. When there was a suggestion box on the office door, it was always empty. But when our new president changed the sign on it to "Criticisms", it was suddenly overflowing.'

Once again, Benson's garden had been trampled on by rampaging children and he gazed at the damage with dismay.

'I'm afraid there's not much you can do about that,' said his neighbour.

'Oh, yes, there is,' insisted Benson, 'and I know just what to plant to stop those little devils.'

'And what's that?'

'A barbed-wired fence!'

Fred, not the greatest gardener in the world, couldn't stop talking about the honeysuckle vine he'd planted and which, by some sort of miracle, was actually not only growing but thriving.

'Why, do you know,' he was telling a dinner party one evening, 'I swear that thing is growing by leaps and

bounds. If it's grown a foot so far a week it's –'

Suddenly, there was a knock on the door. 'Who on earth can that be?' Fred demanded, annoyed that his story was being interrupted.

'Perhaps, dear,' said his wife sweetly, 'it's your vine.'

At the seed counter of the local garden centre, a bemused novice gardener was heard to say: '. . . and then I covered them up, and that was the last I saw of them.'

'What's the matter, Marge?' a friend asked a glum exhibitor at the garden show.

'Wouldn't you know it,' said Marge. 'I go to all the trouble and expense of bringing these anemones all the way across the county, and what do they do? They hang their heads.'

The very keen amateur gardener was driving through the country when she came across a vast field of many acres of corn ripe for harvesting. 'My,' she said to the bemused farmer, 'you *do* have green fingers!'

The eager, if small-scale, gardener who lived in a penthouse right in the middle of a major city was getting along just fine with his plants in wooden tubs and window boxes and a book on gardening until he read the following instructions: 'Enrich the soil with humus, which can be obtained from any nearby bog . . .'

Old Alf, the grizzled veteran of our gardening club, was warned that he should be very careful around one of our new lady members as she was very shy.

'Mrs Carruthers is bringing some of her prize-winning African violets to the monthly show, Alf,' said the president, 'so take it easy.'

'You know me,' said Alf. 'The soul of discretion.'

But no sooner had Mrs Carruthers nervously set out her exhibitions in the church hall that Alf came roaring in with a hearty: 'All right then, Mrs C. Let's see your bloomers!'

'George,' said his wife from the kitchen, 'will you go and get a vegetable from the freezer for dinner?'

George came in from the garage with a package hand-lettered 'peas', but when he opened the freezer bag, he found it contained a completely different vegetable not the least resembling a pea.

'What's this about, Elsie?' he asked his wife.

'I couldn't remember how to spell "broccoli",' she said.

'Now, you *must* eat up all your vegetables,' insisted the mother of two stubborn children, pointing at their overflowing plates.

When they refused, she turned to her husband for support, but was surprised to find him looking quite cheerful: 'What are you smiling about?' she demanded.

'I'm just thinking how much we're saving by *growing* vegetables they won't touch rather than *buying* them.'

'Honestly, Rupert,' said the keen gardener's wife, 'I know you've got an all-out campaign against greenfly this year, but that doesn't mean you have to paint one on the side of your sun hat every time you make a kill.'

AAAAAAAAAGH!

My elderly neighbour finally had to give up taking care of her own lawn and so had to advertise for someone to do the heavy work. But I couldn't help noticing that her usually flawless grass was looking pretty patchy, and that the small boy behind the lawnmower seemed to change every week.

Finally, out of exasperation, she nailed a sign on her front fence: 'Wanted: someone old enough to mow better.'

Every spring Hodgson met Brown in front of the grass seed display at the garden centre. 'Well,' he said as they looked over the vast display of packets of seed, 'what do you think you'll try this year?'

'Crazy paving,' said Brown shortly.

'Right after lunch,' Parkinson told his wife, 'I'm going to start seriously combatting those slugs.'

But half an hour later when she went out to hang up the wash, Mrs Parkinson found her husband lying in a garden chair perfectly still with his eyes closed.

'I thought you were going to get after those slugs, John,' she said.

'I am. I am,' replied her husband, 'but to be really

effective you've got to think like your enemy, so I'm practising.'

The beggar wasn't doing very well until he printed a crude sign and placed it beside his upturned hat on the ground: 'Wife, two children and ornamental garden to support.'

The very keen gardener came home from the big vegetable show walking on air and pinned his newest blue ribbon in the middle of the bulletin board.

'You'd think,' his wife told a neighbour over the garden fence, 'that he'd won the Nobel Peas Prize.'

Griffiths, who tolerated his wife's gardening mania rather than encouraged it, watched with bemusement as course after course arrived on the dinner table. Carrot salad was followed by stew heavily weighed down with carrots followed by delicious but undeniably carroty cake.

After the first bite, he looked up and remarked mildly: 'You kind of got carrot away today, didn't you?'

Perkins was on his back porch preparing cabbages for his roadside stall. Looking around at the litter of outer leaves strewn all around, he asked: 'Where are all of those cabbage moths now that I need them?'

For sale sign on a lawn roller: 'A hundred feet to a gallon (of sweat).'

The visiting expert listened very warily as Mrs Arbuthnot, our club's most struggling gardener, described the difficulties she was experiencing with her garden.

'What would you recommend that I plant,' she asked, 'in an area which is half clay and half rock, with extremely high acidity, subjected to far too much midday sun and receiving hardly any rainfall?'

The expert scratched his head and finally ventured: 'A flagpole?'

Complaint to a seed company: 'I would not venture to suggest that your service is slow, but the selection of seeds I ordered just arrived in the form of a bouquet.'

A mother and daughter were busily weeding a large garden, and it was clear that the girl wasn't enjoying it a bit.

'I don't understand,' said her mother. 'You used to ask if you could help all the time.'

'Yes,' said the girl, 'but that was before I was big enough to help.'

The motorist stopped at a roadside strawberry stand and asked the very small boy manning it: 'Are the strawberries good this year?'

'I don't know,' said the boy. 'I hate strawberries. That's why Dad gives me this job.'

A Londoner's neighbour from Australia was digging a deep but not very large hole in the middle of his back lawn. 'Digging a swimming pool?' asked his neighbour facetiously.

'Nah,' said the Aussie, 'Going home.'

GARDENER-
THIS IS AN
OFFICIAL
PICKET
PICKET
so please don't
pick it!
BEES
UNION
ZEALOT
ZONE

Have you heard about the threatened strike by the bumblebees? They want shorter flowers and more honey.

The proud gardener completed his display with a carefully lettered sign: 'Fronds and Anemones' and stood back to reflect in the glory he was sure they would attract.

'Your fronds really are most magnificent,' said a friend. 'I don't think I've ever seen their like. Such colours and delicate leaf patterns,' he marvelled. 'But, I hope you'll pardon my asking where your anemones are? I don't seem to see them anywhere.'

'Richard,' said the proud horticulturist with an expansive gesture, 'I'm surprised at you even asking. With fronds like *these*, who needs anemones?'

Despite all their best efforts, the Parkinsons' flower beds were a dismal failure. Their poppys were dwarflike, their daffodils spindly, their roses a brown-leafed disgrace.

'I suppose we'll just have to forget about them this year,' said Mr Parkinson.

'I'm going to try one last thing,' said his wife, taking her trowel and beginning to dig carefully around the roots of a towering dandelion in a patch of weed.

'Whatever are you doing?'

'I'm giving our rotten flowers,' she said grimly, 'something to set them a good example.'

The customers in the check-out queue at the gardening shop were surprised to see a middle-aged patron at the front of the queue hold a deck chair he was carrying high over his head and say loudly to the girl behind the cash register: 'I'm buying this very comfortable chair for myself. Not for anyone else in my family to use. For myself, only!'

They thought he was being very eccentric, indeed, until the check-out girl rang up the purchase and said, 'Are you going to pay cash, Dad?'

Sign on the garden stall at our local market: 'All Prices reduced. This is Your Chance to Catch Us with Our Plants Down.'

It was the last day of autumn, and Mrs Griggs found her husband down at the bottom of the garden under the oak tree standing by a huge pile of leaves, rake in hand and apparently gazing blankly into space.

'Howard,' she demanded, 'what on earth are you doing?'

'Waiting,' he said grimly, pointing skyward at a single red-brown leaf trembling all alone at the top of the tree.

'Well, darling,' said the excited first-time gardener, 'I think I'm all ready to start. I've got spade, fork, seeds, fertiliser and watering can. Can you think of anything else I need?'

'Learner plates?' enquired his wife sweetly.

'Arthur,' insisted the gardener's wife, 'for the very last time, you'll *have* to make a scarecrow. You can't expect mother to stand out there in your garden *all* day.'

'George is very generous,' sighed the gardener's wife, 'but sometimes I wish he would try to surprise me just a little when he buys me a present.'

'What do you mean?' asked her friend.

'Well, as much as he tries, it's very hard to disguise a gift-wrapped pitchfork.'

THE GARDEN CYNIC'S DICTIONARY OF DEFINITIONS:

ANNUAL: Any plant which only comes up once, including many perennials.

BED (FLOWER): Anywhere a dozen or more seeds happen to land.

CATALOGUE (SEED): A work of fiction with fantastic photographs.

CRABGRASS: Crop from seed which you can't buy and which money can't get rid of.

FENCE: The object which usually separates you from really good soil.

FERTILISER: Nature's way of notifying a change in the wind direction.

FRUIT CROP: Anything in excess of what the birds, insects and neighbourhood children can eat.

FURROW: Not necessarily the shortest distance between two points; often found in forehead of gardener.

GARDEN: Another name for purgatory.

GARDENER: A masochist who is in no hurry.

GREEN FINGERS: The unique ability to combine weather, soil and luck.

HOE: Instrument of torture not thought to be readily available to the Spanish Inquisition.

MULCH: Improving the soil by means God would have used if he'd known of a good garden centre.

NURSERY: A place to buy plants with a life span exactly as long as the drive home.

PERENNIAL: This year, possibly; next year, unlikely.

PEST: The gardener next door.

PLANT (TO): A variation of the verb: TO BURY.

POTATO: Fast food for next entry.

POTATO BEETLE: A sure solution to the problem of your own personal food mountain.

ROSE PLANT: Housing project for greenfly.

ROT: The gardeners' universal tongue.

SEED: Tiny objects with high prices and low yields.

SPADE: Highly efficient blister-making machine.

STAKE: What garden centre owners ought to be burned at.

WEED: Perfect example of Darwin's theory of 'Survival

of the Fittest'.

YARD: Someone else's garden.

ZITHER: What any sensible person would be lying in a hammock playing rather than gardening.

'You know,' said the keen gardener at a dinner party, 'I'm feeling very cheerful tonight. Just this afternoon I had several tons of nice, ripe manure delivered for my garden.'

'I feel pretty cheerful myself,' said the man on his left.

'What about?' asked the puzzled gardener.

'That I don't live next door to you.'

The reluctant gardener arrived home after work to find a note from his wife: 'Your dinner is in the oven. Cook at gas mark 6 for *exactly* the amount of time it takes you to mow the back lawn.'

The scene was one of total devastation. Weeks of rainfall had pushed the river over its banks, and the water had risen to window height. But as the police rowed up to one householder marooned on his

roof, they found him smiling broadly.

'I hope you don't mind me asking, sir,' said the police sergeant, 'but why are you so cheerful?'

'Tomorrow,' smiled the flood victim, 'I was finally going to start weeding my garden.'

Definition of a sadist: a garden centre proprietor who sells you a wheelbarrow, loads it with a hundred weight of fertiliser, fifty pounds of peat, ten pounds of seed, fork, spade, watering can and adds on top a book called 'Gardening Made Easy'.

'I thought I told you to start digging the garden,' the father told his teenaged son.

'What?' said the boy, 'and get charged with disturbing the ecology?'

Complaining father: 'My daughter's idea of helping to make our garden beautiful is to lie on our sun-lounger and work on her tan.'

From the garden club bulletin board:

My cabbages are pinched and mean
My radishes keep dying
You wouldn't think my runner beans
Are hardly even trying
I try to pretend indifference
And tell the world: 'Who needs it?'
But my garden knows its guilty
Of biting the hands that weeds it.

'Do you think, Perkins, it's true that things grow better if you talk to them?' Blake called over to the man on the next allotment.

'I doubt it,' said Perkins. 'Alma's been talking to me non-stop for 35 years, and I haven't grown an inch.'

The old gardener watched silently as his lady neighbour, a rank newcomer, planted several dozen bulbs, and when she looked up, he'd taken off his flat cap and was standing at attention with the cap held over his heart.

'Whatever are you doing, Mr Hardy?' she asked finally.

'Showing respect,' said the old man. 'You just

planted them bulbs so darned deep that it's the least I could do, considering.'

Jones was standing on a stepladder at the edge of his garden for a long time with the hedge-cutters in his hand when his wife called out: 'Bert, you'd better warn Miss Boddy not to lie out in the sun too long, she'll get burnt.'

'How do you know she's sunbathing?' Jones said with a scarlet face, looking down at his wife.

'Well, dear,' Mrs Jones said, 'you've been on that one spot for fifteen minutes, and besides, that's a fence, *not* a hedge.'

The nursery customer was very particular about the tree she wanted for her garden. 'Now,' she insisted, 'I want to plant something which will throw lots of shade, but not too much. It must be full and bushy in the summer but allow sun to shine in our windows in the winter. And above all it mustn't drop leaves all over the place for me to rake up in the autumn. Is that clear?'

The nurseryman scratched his head for a while.

'Leave it to me,' he said.

When the customer got home late that afternoon she found standing proudly in the middle of her garden – a large umbrella.

The Caldecotts were all ready to leave on holiday. The luggage was stacked in the hallway, passports, travellers cheques and tickets were checked and rechecked, the taxi to the airport was outside, when Mrs Caldecott, her hand on the doorknob, suddenly remembered something.

'Just one second, Bruce,' she told her husband, and rushed toward her greenhouse.

When she got there, she told her plants: 'Now, don't be alarmed if a stranger comes in. It'll only be Mrs Pratt from number 37. She's going to look in on you while we're away, and she couldn't be nicer.'

'You look worried,' said one Fairy Godmother to another as they met at their club. 'What's the problem?'

'Where the hell,' asked the other, 'am I going to get an *organic* pumpkin?'

'You're going to have to build a bigger pest-proof bird table, dear,' said the wife looking out into the garden.

'Why's that?' asked her husband.

'Well, it only holds six squirrels, and the rest can't seem to get on.'

Hokanson, the gardening club's deadbeat – the one who was always borrowing seeds and then trying to sell his produce – was strenuously negotiating with a farmer over the price of a load of fine, rotted horse manure for a full hour before he beat the price down to a level to suit him.

Finally, the farmer wearily agreed to Hokanson's price and dumped the ripe load. 'I'll send you a cheque tomorrow,' Hokanson shouted as the farmer drove off.

'I just don't understand,' said old Barstow, who'd overheard them bargaining, 'why you wasted all that time when we both know you're not going to pay him anyway.'

'Don't be silly,' Hokanson remonstrated. 'Old Giles is a very good man, and it can't be easy supporting his family on that terrible land of his. He can't afford to take on any large unrecoverable debts as well.'

Stout went into the ironmongers to buy a new pitchfork, but he found there were none in stock.

'I'm sorry,' said the ironmonger, 'we're expecting a shipment in next week. In the meantime, can I sell you a spade? I've got a great selection.'

'I'll say you have,' said Stout, noticing that the shop was practically bulging with hundreds and hundreds of spades of every kind and make. 'You must sell a lot of spades.'

'Me?' said the ironmonger. 'I hardly sell one from week to week. But the rep who sold me all these, boy, can *he* sell spades!'

'Your problem,' said the gardening expert sternly to the downcast amateur, 'is that you like your runner beans all right, but you don't *love* them.'

Who was the first gardener?
Adam.
What were his first words?
'Typical. All this weeding to do, and where's everybody gone?'

PUNS BY THE PUNNET:
'When are you going to cut the shrubbery?' she asked sharply.

'Soon,' he hedged.

The new member of the local gardening club found everybody very friendly until he attended a social evening and noticed one group of members kept very much to themselves in one corner and seemed to make all the others nervous.

'Who on earth are they?' he asked a friendly chap at the bar.

'Them?' said his new friend. 'I'd be very careful if I were you, that's the Gardening Mafia.'

'Gardening Mafia?'

'Yes. If you get on the wrong side of them, they send the boys around to criticise your runner beans.'

At the local pub, one chap nudged another and said: 'Here. You see that bloke in the corner, the one with a complexion like a beet?'

'What about him?'

'He must be the unluckiest man alive.'

'How so?'

'Well, he's the president of our local Horticultural Society, specialising in cultivating wild mushrooms and has been widowed three times. His first two wives died of mushroom poisoning, poor chap.'

'What did his third wife die of?'

'A fractured skull. Apparently she wouldn't eat her mushrooms.'

Sign on the back of the florist's delivery van: 'Warning: this vehicles makes fragrant unexpected stops.'

When it came to his turn, the garden shop customer asked the assistant: 'Do you have any weed seeds?'

'I'm afraid we don't sell them, sir,' said the assistant. 'If you don't mind me asking, what do you want them for?'

'Well,' said the customer, 'every year I plant seeds for vegetables, soft fruit and flowers but all I get is weeds, but this year I'm going away for a holiday so I thought I'd save time by skipping the initial stages.'

Carter took delivery of a yearling peach tree on an unseasonably hot spring day but wanted to wait for cooler weather to plant it, so he asked the men from the nursery to put the tree on his son's little red wagon. This meant he was also able to roll the tree around his fairly spacious back garden looking for the ideal place to plant it eventually. While he was absorbed in this delicate matter, Carter noticed that Rusty, his Old English sheepdog, was following him around, panting heavily from the heat. Taking the hosepipe, he liberally sprinkled the grateful dog.

Hearing loud laughter, he looked up to find his next-door neighbour leaning over the fence. 'Now I've seen it all,' said the neighbour. 'I've actually witnessed someone who walks his tree and waters his dog.'

Overnight, it seemed, it became the neighbourhood fad for people to give their gardens names. Ferguson tacked 'Sans Souci' over his garden gate; O'Brien opted for 'Floral Delight', and Mrs Smith picked the name: 'Waterside', to celebrate her expensive new pond.

'I'm beginning to feel left out,' Harold told his wife. 'What do you think I ought to call *my* garden?'

Casting an eye over his less than magnificent spread, she suggested: 'Death Row?'

Feeling fed up with an unending round of housework one Saturday, the housewife made her husband, a less than enthusiastic gardener, an offer he couldn't refuse.

'If you'll do my work for the rest of the day, I'll do yours.'

He agreed, and settled happily down in a deck chair while his wife began mowing their large front garden. But they soon both became aware that their agreement was attracting less than favourable attention from the neighbours. The shaking of heads, tut-tutting and pointed looks in the husband's direction made it difficult for either of them to enjoy their agreement.

'I've got it,' said the wife finally. She jumped in her car and roared away. In less than half an hour, she was back and resumed her mowing. The major difference was that she was then wearing a bright, yellow T-shirt bearing the legend, front and back: 'DON'T WORRY; HE DOES THE DISHES.'

The guest speaker at our garden club was nervous. 'I'm very glad to be here,' he said to the chairwoman, 'but I don't want to talk too long and bore everyone. How will I know when I've talked too long?'

'Well, it's hard to say,' said the chairwoman, 'but usually when a speaker begins to think his talk is really getting interesting, that's about time to start winding up.'

The executive dropped by the home of his boss, an avid gardener, at the weekend to discuss some business matter when he noticed a great strapping fellow – at least six feet, six inches tall and broad with it – carrying a hundred-weight bag of fertiliser into the back garden as if it were a feather pillow.

'Who's *that*?' the executive asked.

'Oh,' said the boss dismissively, 'that's just the little man who helps us in the garden.'

'What's the meaning of this?' demanded the father when he found his carefully tended garden full of his teenager daughter's friends dancing to a loud and raunchy band.

'Well, Daddy,' she said sweetly, 'you did say you were thinking of having a rock garden.'

At the garden shop, the proprietor had been having a terrible time shifting a new type of hoe he'd ordered, but one Saturday when Joe came in he found that they'd all been sold.

'How the heck did you do that?' Joe asked wonderingly.

'Simple,' said the shopkeeper. 'I just put a sign on them: "Only one to a customer." '

The rather posh gardening club had a strict dress code which forbade the wearing of denims of any kind by members. There was considerable surprise, then, when on a weekend morning one of the younger and comelier female members of the club turned out in extremely form-fitting Levis.

'Really,' complained one veteran lady member to the club president, looking pointedly in the direction of the offender who was bending over her plants, oblivious of the scandal she was causing. 'One must keep up club standards, mustn't one?'

'Assuredly, my dear lady,' said the president,

admiring the view rather too openly, 'but I think in this case you must admit that the end justifies the jeans.'

'I've heard of fly-eating plants,' said the customer to the assistant at the nursery, 'but can you suggest anything I could plant in my garden which might be a bit more ambitious?'

'Ambitious? How do you mean, sir?'

'I was rather thinking of the ten-year-old boy who lives next door to me.'

Hand-printed sign over a stand selling home-made strawberry preserves: 'If we hadn't been found in the same bed, we wouldn't be in this sort of a jam.'

The gardener went out among his vegetables and found that snails had riddled his crop of fine, young lettuces. Returning to the house, he found his worried-looking wife waiting for him.

'For God's sake, Elsie,' he snapped. 'Don't just stand there. Counter my pessimism!'

The large and rather impressive-looking anniversary present from Aunt Agatha arrived, but when the wrapping was removed it turned out to be an exceedingly ugly plastic garden gnome.

'I do wish,' said the husband, 'that Aunt Agatha wouldn't insist on giving us something we don't already have.'

At the breakfast table, Mrs Poindexter looked in vain for the expected silver anniversary present and then asked her husband with carefully controlled impatience: 'Concentrate, George. Can't you think of *anything* really important which happened exactly twenty-five years ago today?'

George scratched his chin in bewilderment, then suddenly smiled: 'Of course! Of course! That was the day I was elected president of the gardening society.'

On safari on darkest Africa, Merriwhether accidentally stepped on the foot of an ancient crone as he was walking through a native marketplace. Despite his apologies, she pointed a withered and pointed finger at him and shrieked: 'May your house burn down; may your business fail; may your bones all

break; may your roses be infested with greenfly!'

'We'd better leave,' said their guide, hustling the Merriwhethers away. 'She's quite a famous witch doctor in these parts.'

For the rest of the day, Merriwhether was unusually subdued and quiet, and finally his wife spoke up: 'Surely, Martin,' she said, 'you didn't take that old woman seriously? You can't believe in black magic.'

'I don't know, Madge,' he said worriedly. 'I didn't like the sound of that bit about the greenfly.'

'I think it's a good idea of yours to move the garden inside this year,' said Mrs Badderly.

'What on earth are you talking about?' demanded her husband. 'My garden is going to be where it's always been.'

'It's a natural mistake to make, Ralph,' she said. 'What else was I to think after you tracked most of the topsoil onto my kitchen floor?'

'Mr Garroway to see you,' the secretary told the editor.

The editor looked up from a manuscript to find Garroway standing in front of his desk dressed in green

Wellingtons, mud-streaked overalls, straw hat, with hoe and pitchfork over his shoulder and a watering can in his hand.

'Tell me, Mr Garroway,' the editor asked, 'what sort of book have you written?'

As the debate at the gardening society meeting got more and more heated, one enthusiastic gardener asked another: 'How can you mention *Eucharis grandiflora "amazonica"*, *Astranta umbelliferae* and *Echinacea palida* in the same breath?'

The gardener wasn't having much luck selling produce from the stall next to his driveway until he had the bright idea of putting up a sign: LAST HOME-GROWN, ORGANIC, LOVINGLY NURTURED PRODUCE BEFORE THE MOTORWAY.

'What'll it be?' the pub landlord asked Jenkins, a keen gardener.

'Make it a double, John,' said Jenkins. 'It was hell in the trenches this afternoon!'

Did you hear about the suburban Gardening Club and the local Amateur Dramatics Society which combined their efforts to do a production of 'Mulch Ado About Nothing'?

The young stockbroker and the garden centre assistant were bent for the longest time over the catalogue. 'Are you *sure*,' demanded the stockbroker, 'that this particular vine is upwardly mobile?'

Woman after buying a vast amount of equipment and material at a garden centre: 'It all came to much more than I thought it would, but then I thought it might.'

Sign over a display of new spades at a suburban garden centre: 'Don't heave loam without one.'

Jack was cock-a-hoop over winning the prize for the biggest potatoes in the show and couldn't help rubbing it in.

'Well, Ernie, old pal,' he crowed to his neighbour, 'didn't have much luck with your spuds this year, eh?

GULP
Happy Birthday

A bit stunted, weren't they?'

'You could say that,' retorted Ernie, 'but I grew them to fit *my* mouth, not *yours*.'

The customer at the garden centre was lingering so long over his selection of a new wheelbarrow that the assistant went over to see if she could help.

'I've just about made up my mind,' the customer told her. 'It's between this one with the deep bed and the red one with the ball-wheel.' Finally, he chose the red one, and as the assistant was ringing up the purchase, apologised: 'I'm so sorry to dither so, but you see, it's a present for my wife's birthday.'

'Will it be a surprise?' asked the assistant.

'I rather think so,' he said. 'She expects a pearl necklace.'

After a big argument about organic versus non-organic techniques, about half of the local gardening club quit and founded their own on the other side of the village.

Despite the row, the presidents of the two clubs

remained on speaking terms – just. When they met in the street, the president of the old club said to the leader of the new in a condescending tone of voice: 'I say, Basil, I passed your clubhouse the other day.'

'That's very kind of you, Percy,' said Basil swiftly.

Old Trevor, the Horticultural Society patriarch, allowed himself to be dragged to church one rainy Sunday morning, and the vicar was expatiating on the symbolism of the dove.

'Tell me,' he asked his congregation, 'what do you think of when you see a dove?' When nobody answered, he urged them: 'Oh, surely, you must have some automatic associations you attach to the lovely, white dove.'

'Gentleness,' called out a parishioner.

'Purity,' said another.

Trevor couldn't restrain himself: 'Eats my blasted Brussels sprouts!' he shouted from the back pew.

The manager of the garden centre came out of his office to hear Jenkins, one of his most trusted assistants, saying to a lady customer: 'No madam, we certainly haven't had any for some time,

and Lord knows when we will get any.'

When the customer had gone, the manager tackled him: 'I heard that, Jenkins,' he remonstrated, 'and I must say that I am surprised at you. Never, never admit to a customer that we can't get them something. That's what we're here for. If it's out of stock, tell her you'll get it for her soon. Now, what was it, the lady wanted?'

'Rain,' said Jenkins quietly.

Brewster, a relatively new gardener, believed in doing everything by the book, and would not make a move in his garden without consulting one of his many gardening manuals.

That year, he'd grown an especially impressive marrow which he planned to enter in a show, and he didn't want to take any chances when he cut the marrow from its vine. So, with secateurs in one hand and Marrow Manual in the other, he was kneeling over the massive squash when his next-door neighbour glanced over the fence.

'What are you doing?' asked the neighbour, 'reading it its rights?'

The fanatical gardener sat in the doctor's waiting room with his hat firmly on his head. When at last his turn came, he whipped the hat off to reveal a rose plant growing from the top of his head.

The astonished physician didn't know what to say. Finally he said: 'That's amazing, but I don't know what you expect *me* to do.'

'Call yourself a doctor?' roared the gardener. 'Can't you see that I'm riddled with greenfly?'

Parsons' garden was tucked in the corner where two footpaths met, and walkers couldn't seem to resist taking a shortcut across his vegetable patch until he put up a big sign: 'Trespassers are requested not to disturb the adders.'

The neighbours began to notice that Simpkins, not content just to have a pile of manure at the end of his plot, had begun to shape the stuff into a very careful pyramid of impressive dimensions. 'I'm beginning to think,' said one of them, 'that Simpkins has got Pharaohs at the bottom of his garden.'

ROOT OF A GROWING PROBLEM

Mrs Blakeney laid everything out for a special candlelit supper, took a long bath and then carefully applied her most expensive and exotic perfume.

When he heard her call, Blakeney came into the house, took one sniff and said: 'Summer really is coming on. I notice you've started to use the flyspray.'

'Sometimes George drives me mad,' said the gardener's wife, 'but I have to admit that he's the only labour-saving device I know of that you can cuddle.'

The eager gardener had his tools all over the sitting room floor getting them ready for the first assault of spring on his garden when his wife looked out of the window and asked: 'Philip, don't you think it might be a bit early to start gardening?'

'Why's that?' her husband asked without looking up from his task.

'Well, there's a penguin on our bird table.'

Bertha had been debating with herself for days what to plant on the trellis in her back garden when finally she made up her mind. 'I'm going to plant jasmine,' she told her husband, 'just for the smell of it.'

Powell was very proud of his prize-winning tomatoes and was upset when one night about half of his crop disappeared from his garden. But he told no one about the losses, and a couple of weeks later, Oakeshott, a near neighbour, asked him: 'Did you ever find out who was stealing your tomatoes?'

'Not until just now,' replied Powell.

More up-to-date members of the club brought in the most outlandish gardening gadgets to work their plots, but old Figgis, the oldest member, said he'd stick with fork, spade and hard work. 'As I see it,' he said, 'there's basically three types of gardening gimmicks: those that don't work; those that break down and those that get lost.'

Said one cavewife to another about her husband: 'Sometimes I wish he'd go back to hunting. Ever since he started putting those seeds in the ground, all he does is complain about the weather.'

Grannie Brown was kneeling in the middle of her garden when a stranger called to her over the fence: 'What are you growing?'

'Older,' came the prompt reply.

Osborn, one of the most taciturn of the gardening club's members, was seen one day spreading newspapers between the rows of his vegetable garden.

'What are you doing?' asked a friend.

'I know it's all the rage,' said Osborn, 'but I can't find anything to say to my plants, so I'm giving them something to read instead.'

WEED KILLER
SEED PACK

THE WORLD'S TEN MOST USELESS GARDENING QUESTIONS:

Did you grow that yourself?
What do you find to *say* to your plants?
What did that tomato actually *cost* you to grow?
Do you *enjoy* weeding?
Are those vegetables really organic?
Are you self-sufficient in snapdragons?
Which of you wears the trousers in the garden?
Is it hot enough for you?
If you planted the bulbs the wrong way down, would they come up in China?
Do you really like swedes that much?

The scourge of the gardening society was old Doctor Rankin, who made a point of trying to get *personally* acquainted with every pretty new female member.

'My dear,' he said to a young beginner, cornering her in the society shop, 'how ever do you keep that absolutely glorious shape?'

'Well, for a start, *doctor*,' she said with emphasis, 'I eat an apple a day.'

At the garden show, Mrs Fulcher was looking over the power mowers with a view to buying one for her husband.

'I'm especially worried about reliability,' she told the salesman. 'I wouldn't want to get one which would be breaking down all the time.'

'I assure you, madam,' said the salesman with a touch of hauteur, 'a mower this expensive *never* breaks down. If anything, it will *malfunction.*'

The apartment dweller bought a vast number of potted plants, but wasn't having much luck with them.

'I water them, I feed them, I spray them,' she complained to a friend. 'I even *talk* to them, but I can't help thinking they're laughing up their leaves at me.'

During a serious drought, local gardeners found themselves restricted by a hosepipe ban and had to make every spare drop of water count. They were wondering if their crops would just shrivel up and die, when suddenly a heavy rain began to pour from the sky practically flooding the parched gardening plots.

'You know,' said the club philosopher, 'if this rain

keeps up, we just might be allowed to use hosepipes again.'

The distraught housewife met the neighbourhood handyman at the door wringing her hands: 'I'm afraid that our power mower has water in its carburettor.'

'No problem,' he said. 'I can get it going. Where is it?'

'Well,' she said, 'just at this moment it's at the bottom of our pond.'

Richardson looked out of the window and saw his neighbour, a professional writer, hard at work in his garden. Toward the end of the morning, he wandered out and found the profusely sweating author taking a short break.

'Not writing, then?' Richardson asked.

'No,' said his neighbour, wiping his brow, 'I thought I'd take a rest today.'

Letter to a gardener from a seed company: 'Dear Account No. 325789: As you know, we at Acme Seeds and Bulbs like to cultivate the personal touch . . .'

A horticultural lecturer was advising a new member of the faculty on his technique for taking students on field trips. 'Myself,' he concluded, 'I always wear boots a couple of sizes too big.'

'Whatever for?' asked the new man.

'So I can hide any specimens I don't recognise before the students see them and start asking questions.'

Two strangers in a pub struck up a conversation, and their talk turned to maintaining a happy marriage.

'I'm a firm believer in sharing the wealth,' said one. 'If a man comes into some unexpected money, I think he ought to go out and buy his wife the most expensive house plant he can afford.'

'Not a bad idea,' said the other. 'Are you a marriage guidance counsellor?'

'No, I'm a florist.'

The new gardening club member, a high-powered businessman, was amazed at the seeming serenity of old Jeff, a senior member.

'Frankly,' the new member told him, 'I started gardening as a contrast to my pressurised business life, but I'm not finding it easy to make the transition, especially when the weather is bad and I can't work in my garden. How on earth do you stay so tranquil all of the time?'

'Well,' said Jeff, drawing on his pipe, 'I learned a long time ago that when it wants to rain, the best thing to do is just to go ahead and let it.'

The important-looking matron past the slimness of youth put in her order at the garden centre counter and waited. But customer after customer seemed to be receiving their purchases while there was no sign of hers. Finally, she could bear it no longer and called out: 'I hope you haven't forgotten me. I'm the wheelbarrow with the inflated ball wheel.'

The man living next to a family with many, many children put a large sign up in the middle of his garden: 'IT IS DANGEROUS FOR CHILDREN

TO ENTER THIS GARDEN!!!'

Finally, the man next door, the father of the many progeny, couldn't resist asking his neighbour: 'What's so dangerous?'

'Me!' said the gruff gardener.

Sign in a suburban nursery: 'Please do not talk to our plants unless you plan to buy them.'

Harkins had just finished digging a deep soakaway smack in the middle of his garden when the little boy from next door looked through the mesh fence and asked him: 'Did *you* do that?'

'Yes,' said Harkins with not a little pride.

'Boy, are you going to catch it,' said the boy.

The student asked his teacher: 'Sir, what causes rain?'

'Well, Thompkins,' said the teacher, who was a keen gardener, 'the principal causes of rain are low-pressure areas, cold fronts, warm, moist air and weekends!'

'How on earth do you maintain such a huge garden?' the neighbourhood newcomer asked Parsons, admiring his acres of neat rows of crops.

'Well,' said Parsons, 'I use three basic methods for getting a job done: do it myself, employ someone to do it or forbid my children to do it.'

After hearing her father say many, many times that he couldn't afford to buy a new sit-upon lawnmower, the little girl was surprised one Saturday morning when a man delivered a splendid brand-new mower.

'But, Daddy,' asked the little girl, 'who gave us the money to buy it?'

'The bank, darling,' said her father.

'That was nice of them,' said the girl. 'But how are you going to thank them?'

'Monthly, dear,' said her father. 'Monthly.'

At a football match, the man in the front row kept shouting: 'Easy, Bill! Take it easy, Bill! Don't get hurt!'

After quite a bit of this, a woman in the second row asked him: 'Is Bill your son?'

'No,' said the man, 'he's the boy next door, but he promised to mow my lawn tomorrow.'

Sign over a nursery cash register: 'Take home a smile; we have laurel and hardy plants.'

Peters took up an invitation to visit his friend, Davies, who was working in his garden. Peters was surprised to find that plot was closely shadowed on either side by a spur of a motorway and had a flyover arching right over it.

'I have to admire your success under these circumstances,' Peters said. 'What is the most important lesson you would say you have learned from gardening on this site?'

Davies thought long and hard. Then he spoke: 'Never get in a bitter, personal argument with a highway planner.'

When Higson, the jobbing gardener, presented his bill, he couldn't help noticing that it was not greeted with approval.

'Be fair,' he said to the customer. 'You really liked

my estimate. You can't expect everything to come out exactly to your taste.'

The biggest tree in the orchard was holding forth for all of the saplings around it: 'You see,' he expounded, 'it's not how many annual rings you have, so much as how many annual rings you *feel* you have.'

Murphy hired a contractor to dig fifteen holes for fence posts along the boundary of his property, but the contractor found that he was able to get completely around the area to be fenced with only twelve holes.

'That's okay,' said Murphy. 'Just dig the other three over by the porch, and I'll put them where I need them later.'

Graves had spent a long afternoon carefully laying a beautiful pavement along the front of his garden only to find a child tramping footprints along its entire length.

'Get out of it, you little blighter!' Graves cried, taking a swipe at the child.

'Why, Mr Graves,' said the boy's mother. 'I thought you like children.'

'I do. I do,' said Graves. 'But only in the abstract, not in the concrete.'

The proud owner of a brand-new and lavishly stocked garden pool was enjoying his new possession when he suddenly looked into its depths with alarm: 'Betty! Betty!' he cried. 'Come quick! The reduced price one is trying to eat the really expensive one!'

'Henry's been a very keen gardener all of his life,' said his wife with a heavy sigh, 'but I can't deny that sometimes it seems longer.'

Gus, the garden society grump, never had a positive word to say about his garden's progress, no matter what. It was always too wet, too dry, too windy or too still, and he blamed conditions for his rather mediocre vegetables.

But one year everything came out right. The weather was exquisite, and the resulting produce was

undeniably perfect.

'Well, Gus,' teased a member, 'you have to admit that your garden did you proud this year.'

'Suppose so,' said Gus begrudgingly, 'but results like these don't half take it out of the soil.'

Pearson swore by the month-by-month gardening guide until he came upon the following entry: 'Now is the time of the year when the bulbs you forgot to plant last autumn will fail to come up.'

Old Ida was a good customer of the local plant nursery, but at the same time a very difficult one. Time after time, she rang up to complain about a plant which did not meet her exacting standards, and time after time the nursery man wearily took the plant back.

One day the telephone in the nursery rang. 'Hello,' said a voice, 'this is Ida, and . . .'

'I'll be right there,' said the nurseryman. When he arrived, he asked 'What's the problem?'

'There!' said Ida, pointing to an azalea she'd bought recently.

'Why, what's wrong with it?' asked the puzzled

nurseryman. 'It's flourishing.'

'Well, yes,' admitted Ida, 'but *just*.'

Two gardeners were laboriously turning over earth in a garden which had been neglected for many years.

Finally, one of them stopped, wiped his brow and asked: 'I don't suppose there's any danger of *this* work being automated.'

The newlyweds began their first garden with excitement. Carefully, they dug and cleared the ground, scattered the fertiliser, raked it over and lovingly planted the seeds. No sooner had they put the last seed in the ground than the front bell rang, and they both answered the door. It was a salesman.

'As gardeners,' he said, taking in their work clothes and the tools they still held, 'you'll of course be thinking of a chest-type freezer to hold all of your produce.'

'Why, what's the matter, Madge?' Elsie asked her friend when they met at the supermarket.

'It's Fred and our new giant cactus,' Madge said tearfully. 'They have nothing to say to each other.'

Spring had well and truly sprung, and the whole family gathered in the garden to discuss their horticultural plans.

'I'm going to plant peas this year,' said mother.

'Me for red onions and new potatoes,' said father.

'Carrots,' piped up little June.

'I think I'll try haricot vert,' said Arthur, who was studying French at university.

'What about you, Grandfather?' asked June, noticing that the old man hadn't spoken up. 'What are you going to plant?'

'Myself,' said Grandfather firmly, 'in this deck chair and watch all of you work.'

The weather had no sooner begun to warm up a little than Hokanson got out all of his tools and seed catalogues and began to plan his garden.

'I know it's still winter,' he told his wife, 'but if we're going to have plenty of delicious, home-grown produce on our table this summer, we've got to get going right now.'

But then Hokanson noticed that his wife, dressed in her newest frock, was applying new make-up in front of the mirror. 'What are *you* doing?' he asked.

'I agree with you entirely,' said Mrs Hokanson, 'so I'm going to go over and start being especially nice to Mr Jennings, next door.'

Sign over the weedkiller display at the garden centre: 'Give a weed an inch, and it will take a yard.'

Farmer Brown believed in the power of advertising, so a half mile from his new produce stand he erected a huge sign: 'FRESH CORN.'

Then a quarter mile along, he placed another sign: 'FRESH CORN.'

Finally, 200 yards before the stall be built a final

sign: 'FRESH CORN.'

Came the big day and Farmer Brown opened for business, a car came along the highway and pulled off in front of the stand. 'Excuse me,' asked the motorist, 'is the corn fresh?'

The retired boxer took up gardening but found he had a severe case of black fingers. Nothing thrived under his fell hand.

'Sometimes,' he told a friend dispiritedly, 'I feel like throwing in the trowel.'

THE TEN COMMANDMENTS OF GARDENING:

Thou shalt not covet thy neighbours titanium-bladed spade
Thou shalt not believe seed catalogue illustrations
Thou shalt not sneer at thy neighbour's attempt to grow globe artichokes
Thou shalt not try to convince thy children that weeding is 'fun'
Thou shalt not leave surplus lettuces on strangers' porches by night

Thou shalt not smite thy foe with a stem of Brussels sprouts
Thou shalt not try to pass a marrow off as a champion cucumber
Thou shalt not take credit for thy wife's *Molucella laevis*
Thou shalt not set lethal traps for neighbourhood dogs and children
Thou shalt not flaunt thy new mini-tractor.

My wife talks to her hydrangeas for hours and hours.

One day when she was out, I went into the conservatory and asked them: 'How do you stand it?'

'Who listens?' they replied.

'How's your weeping willow?' I asked a member of our gardening circle.

'I'm thinking of asking my doctor to prescribe it an anti-depressant.'

Worried about his raspberry canes, a gardener rang the local television weatherman to enquire

about a predicted strong wind.

'I can't tell you exactly what the wind speed is,' said the weatherman, 'but if it's any help to you, it's just blown our van across the street.'

Mel, the neighbourhood scrounger, wandered into his friend Henry's garden. 'Say, Hank,' he said, 'how about lending me your mower for a couple of hours? My grass is getting so high I can't find the lawn furniture.'

Henry said: 'Sorry, Mel, I'm using it today.'

'All day?' Mel asked.

'That's right.'

'Well, then,' said Mel with a smile, 'you won't mind me borrowing your stepladder then.'

The mother superior called in a tree surgeon to look at the nunnery's ancient and ailing walnut tree.

After carefully examining the tree's leaves and its trunk, the tree surgeon got down on his knees intending to have a look at its roots.

'I don't like to tell you your job,' said the mother

superior, 'but we've been trying *that* approach for weeks.'

'Do you believe that compost stuff is important for healthy soil?' a beginning gardener asked a neighbour.

'Nah, that's a lot of rubbish.'

As the outsiders from the city moved in, the village began to look like a showplace with lovingly restored houses and flamboyant front gardens. They even began to give a weekly award for the best looking garden. Then, one day, a hand-printed sign appeared on the unkept front garden of one of the few remaining locals: 'Lawn of the Weak'.

The ambitious but inexperienced enthusiast found her garden getting in such a mess that she resorted to calling the local jobbing gardener.

'I'll be right over,' he said.

'I'm afraid you'll find me in a dilemma,' she said apologetically.

'That's all right,' said the gardener. 'The last lady that called me was in a kimono.'

Proudly watching their little boy working out in the garden, Mr Brown said to his wife: 'I expect he got his green fingers from me.'

'Probably,' she said. 'I've still got mine.'

While at the garden centre paying for some grass seed he'd ordered to fill in the bald patches in his lawn, Fred noticed a lawnmower he'd fancied for a long time at a very good sale price on the other side of the centre.

'Don't ring that up yet,' he told the assistant. 'I'll be right back.'

When he came back carrying the lawnmower, the assistant said: 'You know, sir, it's the optimistic nature of gardeners like you which makes this job worthwhile.'

'My mother hates onions,' said Gladys, the market gardener's daughter. 'She won't even have one in the house.'

'What about your father?' asked her friend.

'Oh, he can come in,' said Gladys, 'so long as he doesn't bring any onions with him.'

Have you heard about the bonsai tree grower who has been so successful that he is looking for a house with a smaller garden?

Man lying on psychiatrist's couch: 'Doctor, I keep having these dreams that I am being chased by giant, man-eating carrots, sprouts, swedes and radishes with huge, sharp teeth and long tentacles, and no matter where I try to hide, they always find me.'

'I don't want to jump to conclusions so early in your treatment,' said the psychiatrist stroking his beard, 'but by any chance are you a keen gardener?'

The nursery tried a revolutionary sales technique of sending its best customers a video of the new plants it had in stock and inviting them to come into the shop if they saw anything they thought they might like.

Very shortly after, a woman came in and asked to see a large banana tree she'd admired on the video.

When the assistant brought in the plant, she exclaimed: 'I'm amazed! It's even more beautiful in person!'

When grandfather became too fail to tend his considerable garden, the family hired a local jobbing gardener – who happened to be a woman – to come over to the old man's place twice a week and keep his garden in shape.

After a month or so, when one of the grandsons was visiting, he asked: 'What do you think of your gardener, Gramps?'

'Hard to say,' answered the old man. 'He keeps sending his wife.'

'You know,' said the amateur gardener in a southern town, 'the weather is so mild this year, I am tempted to get an early start on my garden.'

'Don't be fooled,' cautioned the veteran. 'Make sure you wait at least until after the two worries.'

'Two worries?'

'Yes,' said the old stager. 'Januworry and Februworry.'

Two visitors to the Chelsea Flower Show were wandering among the exhibitions in awe.

'Isn't that a whatchamacallit plant?' asked one.

'No, I think it's got bigger leaves.'

Bill Brennan, usually at best a very reluctant help to his wife in the garden, was a ball of fire all weekend. He dug, he hoed, he weeded, he wheeled barrows full of manure while his wife Madge sat on the porch. The next Monday morning, the woman next door, asked Madge what on earth had happened to Bill.

'Well,' said Madge, 'Bill read in a magazine article that if a woman isn't so tired she becomes a much better sexual partner, so he volunteered to help me in the garden.'

'I'm not being nosy,' the neighbour said, 'but if you don't mind me asking, was the article right?'

'We don't know yet,' said Madge. 'Bill's been too tired to find out.'

ZZZZZ

'Young man,' demanded the customer at the garden centre, 'will this plant do well in chalky soil?'

'I'm afraid I don't know,' said the man.

A little later she asked him: 'I have a very sunny garden. Could I plant a lobelia there?'

'I've no idea,' said the man. 'I don't work here, you know.'

'I'm not surprised,' said the woman. 'You don't seem to know a thing about gardening.'

'Can anybody tell me what cross-pollination is?' the botany teacher asked her class.

'Please, miss,' said a little girl from the back row, 'is that when the lady flower isn't in the mood?'

The very particular man was buying vegetables at the greengrocer's for his mother-in-law who was of delicate health and insisted on organically grown food. 'They're for my mother-in-law,' he said. 'Have they been sprayed with any poisonous chemicals?'

'Oh, no, sir,' said the greengrocer, 'you'll have to do that yourself.'

Looking over the fence, Higgins asked his neighbour: 'What is that lovely flower? Is it a rose?'

'No. It's a chrysanthemum.'

'Chrysanthemum?' said the puzzled Higgins. 'How do you spell that?'

'K-R-I-S . . . K-H-R-Y . . . no, C-H-Y-R . . .' the neighbour struggled. 'Gosh, you know, it just *might* be a rose after all.'

After three years of hard slog, Perkins finally got the neglected garden backing into the churchyard into good shape and was working in it one day when the new vicar looked over the fence and remarked: 'Your garden is really looking splendid, Mr Perkins. You know, it's wonderful what man and God can do when they work in harmony.'

'Perhaps,' said Perkins, not a fervent churchgoer, 'but you should have seen this garden when God was managing it by himself.'

'That's a wonderful crop of apples you've got there,' Banks shouted to his neighbour, who just happened to be an amateur fortune-teller.

'You think *they're* something?' said the neighbour, 'you should see next year's.'

Blinded by the giant fern plant he is carrying into the exhibition hall, the gardener bumped into an old man and flattened him.

'Oh, I am sorry,' said the gardener, picking the old fellow up and brushing him off.'

'Darn it,' said the angry old man, 'Why can't you just wear a carnation in your buttonhole like everybody else?'

The market gardener sent some handbills to the new convalescent hospital, thinking that he might get some business: 'Sample our fresh fruit and vegetables. You will never get better.'